The Personal Climate Change Handbook

I0442211

Hari Lamba

This HANDBOOK helps you DO Something !

After providing basic information on Global Warming, and what has been done so far to try and solve it, this Handbook informs you on how to become active and what to do:

In your personal life

In your family life

In your Community life

In your State life

In your National life

&

In your Global life

By Harinder (Hari) Lamba
Chicago area

hlamba@sbcglobal.net
hlamba101@gmail.com

Cover Page Acknowledgements – Thanks !
The Water color on the front cover is thanks to the author's brother
Gurvinder (Gobi) Lamba

ISBN-13: 978-1530759538

ISBN-10: 1530759536

Dedications

Dedicated to Suman, Kartik & Katherine

Dedicated to my brother Gurvinder (Gobi) Lamba, whose water color painting adorns the front cover. I appreciate his actions and commitment to our environmental heritage.

Dedicated to all involved in the Climate Change activities worldwide, who have struggled so much and for so long to apply the pressure on the powers to be to make them listen and do what is necessary to address the problem of Climate Change – the greatest challenge that can make or break our Civilization.

I would like to acknowledge the pioneering work of Maurice Strong who worked tirelessly within the UN to further the global environmental agenda and organized the UN Conference on Environment & Development, where the original Climate Change Treaty was signed in 1992 at Rio de Janeiro, Brazil. Debts of gratitude are also due to Al Gore, Rajendra Pachauri and Bill McKibben for their contributions and struggles to the cause of effective change.

This handbook is also dedicated to the Peoples Climate Movement that has taken this struggle to the streets in America. The author has more than a decade, been involved in the activities and conferences of the India Development Coalition of America (IDCA), based in Chicago – their encouragement and support are gratefully acknowledged. The author has gotten involved in supporting the movement, through the efforts of the Sierra Club. It is hoped that this handbook will be an effective tool in the hands of activists and people trying to get actions on solutions to Climate Change. The inspiration of IDCA and the Sierra Club in bringing out this handbook is gratefully acknowledged.

Contents

MESSAGE FROM THE AUTHOR

The good news is that 23 years after the Global Warming Treaty was signed in 1992 at Rio de Janeiro, Brazil, the world finally decided to do something really significant to solve the crisis in Paris on December 12, 2015. But make no mistake, this is the BIGGEST challenge that Global Civilization faces! From being almost totally dependent on fossil fuels, we have to go to being very little dependent on fossil fuels. The challenge is mighty and will take the efforts of everyone big and small – and most importantly – YOU !

So are you ready to use this Handbook and the directions to other resources it provides, to learn and DO what needs to be done, in every aspect of our lives ? If yes, this handbook is for you !

If you think you already know what the problem is and what was agreed to at Paris, then jump straight to Solutions in Chapter 5, which is followed by guidance on what you can do.

FOREWORD

Climate Change represents one of the greatest challenges to global society. It is both a threat and a challenge. The threat is destruction of the life support systems of Planet Earth, on which we all depend, and the challenge is to do this in a relatively short time – in the coming decades. Globally, nationally and individually, what is needed to limit the worst consequences of Global Warming and eventually reduce them. The build-up in the atmosphere of gases emitted by human activity, that trap more and more heat, is having severe consequences which can grow worse – besides temperature rise, there can be sea level rise, increasing ferocity of storm and hurricanes, melting of glaciers and ice, wildfires, drought and extreme flooding – much of which is already happening. The understanding is growing that the solutions are all doable and could be a combination of renewable energy, energy efficiency improvements, and bio-fuels made and used suitably. At the same time, we need to move rapidly to save the carbon sinks (that absorb carbon), namely the global forests, coral reefs, iced masses, and land and coastal ecosystems.

This personal Climate Change Handbook has been prepared so as to provide in one place, a summary of all the things that a reader may need to understand and address the issues of Climate Change, in his or her life, community, state, nation or world.

SUMMARY OF THE PARIS AGREEMENT ON CLIMATE CHANGE

The global Climate Change Conference took place from November 30 to December 11, 2015 in Paris, France, in which 192 nations participated – about 150 presidents and prime ministers were there at the opening. The initial Climate Change Treaty (United Nations Framework Convention on Climate Change, or UNFCC) was signed in Rio de Janeiro in 1992 at the UN Conference on Environment and Development (UNCED – also popularly called the Earth Summit). Thereafter, the Kyoto Protocol (actual action items and binding commitments), arrived in Kyoto, Japan in 1997, had committed developed nations to binding commitments – which has not really succeeded – so something different was needed. The Conference of Parties (COP) consists of those nations that signed the treaty, and their meetings were numbered sequentially, with the activity organized and monitored by the Secretariat in Geneva, Switzerland. The Paris meeting was the 21st meeting, so it was called COP21.

The agreement in Paris provides some basis for hope. The main items agreed to were that the nations would aim for the goal of keeping global temperature rise below 2 degrees C, while trying to keep it below 1.5 degrees C. However, it is estimated that the commitments made at the time of the Paris Agreement is only enough to limit temperature rise to below 3.5 degrees C. The aim was to for the developed nation's emissions to peak soon, with those of developing nations to peak later. The approach was more bottom-up than one mandated from above. Each nation proposed what it would do, and it became what they committed to and how they would do it. Although the goal was $ 100 billion per year contributed by the developed nations to assist developing nations, the year this was to be achieved was extended from 2020 to 2025. Although no liability obligations were agreed to by the richer developed nations, there was agreement that some form of help would be given, especially to low lying island nations for loss and damage caused by global warming. Besides the nations, there were many non-state actors that participated that launched their own initiatives – these included governors, mayors, CEOs and philanthropic billionaires. This was historic agreement that was encouraged by and resulted from the pressure that has built up because of global actions of various people and organizations and by people's movements agitating for change.

The highlights and outcomes were:

1. Each of the nations committed to Nationally Determined Contributions (NDCs) based on what they had proposed themselves – which they committed to implementing domestically. Each nation would continue to report regularly on the progress they are making in achieving their NDCs, and be globally reviewed. These nations cover more than 90% of global emissions, which makes the commitments meaningful.

2. All nations committed to submitting new NDCs every five years, with the hope that they would try to build on the initial NDCs and do better.

3. The richer or developed nations reaffirmed their original treaty commitments and to help the developing nations, many of whom gave commitments for the first time.

4. From a market viewpoint, although the market based approaches like carbon trading did not get direct reference, a new trading mechanism is to be set up to replace Kyoto Protocol's Clean Development Mechanism.

5. The initial taking of stock, or how the nations are progressing will take place in 2018, with nations will be encouraged to start doing better, as presented in new NDCs. A full stock-taking is scheduled for 2023.

6. Agreed to in Paris is a new approach to transparency in which all nations will be required to submit their emissions inventories, and other information so that their progress can be tracked as per their NDCs.

7. It was also agreed that there would be a new mechanism to facilitate and help compliance – as aided by a committee of experts who would facilitate nations – and it would not be adversarial or punitive.

8. In regard to financially helping the poorer developing nations, there was a renewal of commitment by developed nations, and an added commitment by richer developing nations to provide a combination of public and private finance totaling about $ 100 billion a year as a goal up to 2025, and extend it beyond that as a $ 100 b minimum.

9. Then since the bad effects of Global Warming are already under way, and expected to get worse, special attention was paid to Adaptation – so that developing nations hardest hit would be assisted in their adaptation efforts.

10. Also, for loss and damage that might occur due to extreme weather events and slowly developing events like sea rise, developing nations, especially island states would be helped with early warning systems and risk insurance. However, losses and damages incurred would not be used as a basis for liability or compensation.

11. Lastly, the nations will be going back to their home bases and getting domestic approvals, and when approved, would come back for ratification. After at least 55 nations accounting for more than 55% of emissions have signed, then the Agreement would go into force, and regular meetings could be held. In the meantime, and adhoc working group would be formed to take the process forward.

12. On the sidelines, nations offered additional financial pledges of $ 19b. In addition, India and France led 120 nations in forming a Solar Alliance aimed at helping solar energy development in developing nations. About 20 developed and developing nations launched a Mission Innovation initiative for governments to invest in Research and Development of clean energy. Bill Gates and 27 other major investors, worldwide, launched Breakthrough Energy Coalition for private capital investment in clean energy. The Compact of Mayors delivered commitments of over 360 cities to deliver over half of the urban emissions reductions by 2020.

13. France encouraged all of the non-governmental actors to enter their pledges into the NAZCA Portal set up under the Lima-Paris Action agenda. By the time of the Paris meeting, there had been nearly 11,000 commitments entered by non-state actors.

14. The Agreement has been signed by 177 nations, or parties to the agreement. When at least 55 nations representing at least 55% of the global greenhouse gases ratify the agreement (make a formal commitment), the agreement will enter into full force.

The World Resources Institute (WRI) has a very convenient Paris Agreement Tracker where you can monitor the current status on follow-up actions to the Paris Agreement:
http://cait.wri.org/indc/#/ratification

Other organizations should be providing you with updates too – please search online !

Now, the main challenges lie in implementations, actions, monitoring, and financing to make sure that all keep their commitments. The success of the Paris meeting was caused by support from all levels of society.

The success in implementation depends on the continued support and pressure from all levels of society, and YOU !

1. The Effect of Global Warming on the US

Global Warming IS ALREADY Devastating the US

Global warming is not some distant future problem. It has already begun to devastate the US and the world. To understand that, one needs to understand that one of the key things that happen is that when air temperature rises, there is greater evaporation from the sea, and the air has more energy. This leads to two effects, it increases the energy and hence the wind velocity of weather related phenomenon like hurricanes, tornados and coastal storms, while increasing the amount of rain most of the time. We have seen both. The hurricanes are getting stronger and more devastating. Katrina ($ 75 billion losses), Superstorm Sandy ($ 75 billion losses), etc., the list continues to grow. Each time the devastation is greater and the hurricane leaves more damage and grief. Caused by a coastal storm, the recent catastrophic floods in South Carolina (October 2015) are now known to have given one of the highest levels of rainfall in US history, giving 15-19 inches of rain in a 24 hour period ("One in a 1,000 year storm"). Out of 59 sites recording rainfall, six sites set all-time records (NOAA data). In recent years many rainfall events in the Chicago area have led to very high levels of rainfall – some to flash flooding. More and deadlier tornadoes, and severe rainfall events are likely to damage our region. Global warming is not some future problem – its devastation has arrived !

Some of the other Symptoms
1. The melting and disappearance of glaciers – all but a few of Alaska's more than a hundred glaciers are melting and receding.
2. California is facing a persistent and prolonged drought
3. The dry conditions are leading to worse and worse wild fires every year – this could lead to a runaway greenhouse effect – more wild fires, more carbon dioxide in the atmosphere
4. With the mountainsides denuded of vegetation – any rain that follows can cause massive landslides, burying entire communities – this has already happened in the western US
5. The Mississippi Floods of 2005 – high levels of rain and a stationary weather front dumped so much rain that it lead to massive flooding of the Mississippi river

What the Future holds for the US
1. Hurricanes and coastal will get stronger and stronger – devastating coastal areas
2. Tornadoes will get more severe and frequent, and will be felt further north as weather patterns shift – causing untold misery in the America's heartland
3. Floods will go from bad to worse – leading to massive floods as seen in Texas and South Carolina recently.
4. About 2/3rds of Florida will be under water by the end of the century

5. Tropical diseases will become more prevalent as warmer temperatures are felt

2. The Effect of Global Warming on the World

Global Warming IS ALREADY Devastating the World
Do you think that Climate Change will only affect sometime in the future. Think again ! The devastation has already arrived. Coral reefs are where the life on our planet Earth first exploded in the sea, when there was no life on land. Coral reefs when fully alive are the one of the most beautiful places on Earth and where there is enormous diversity of life, like in our Rain Forests. In 1997-98 was the previous global bleaching event when many of the coral reefs bleached (died) because of high ocean temperatures. Some of those have come back a little, especially in non-polluted areas. This year, because of El Nino and hotter sea temperatures, another major global event is predicted, mainly in the Pacific and Indian Oceans.
Some of the other Events/Symptoms
1. Accompanied by the El Nino climate phenomenon, average surface temperatures over sea and land were the hottest during the 2011-2015 years – surface temperature rise is about 0.6 deg. C
2. Hurricanes and Cyclones are getting more and more devastating in all parts of the world- this is because of the increase in temperatures and hence thermal energy in atmosphere.
3. Many parts of the world have experienced yearly increases in temperatures. The summer temperatures in the middle east and in India get hotter every year – leading to increasing deaths caused by heat waves
4. Major floods and occasionally landslides have occurred over the past decade in Honduras
5. Carbon Dioxide concentration in atmosphere was 280 ppm (parts per million) at pre-industrial times – it is now more than 400 ppm.

What the future holds for the World (by the year 2100) *
1. **The most recent assessment indicates that all of these trends have become Extremely Likely ***
    i. There will be higher maximum and minimum temperatures – more hotter days and fewer colder days - This is happening in most parts of the world
  b. Increased frequency, duration and intensity of heat waves
    i. This is getting worse every year in most parts of the world
    ii. Increasing precipitation – meaning much heavier rains, more and more extreme flooding - Recently the large Indian city of Chennai (Madras) suffered a massive rain and flooding unlike ever seen before – most of the city became like islands
  c. Increasing intensity, duration and frequency of cyclones (hurricanes)
    i. Many regions around the world now know and are preparing for hurricanes and cyclones that they expect will be get worse over time.
  d. Increases in extreme sea events – leading to coastal storm of increasing intensity
    i. Most low lying regions like Bangladesh and Florida will be subjected to these large storm surges, before they eventually get submerged after a few decades.

*UN 5th Assessment by Inter-governmental Panel on Climate Change (IPCC) – Several global studies included

3. <u>Chronology of Global Warming Activities</u>

a. In 1896, scientist Arrhenus predicted on principles of Atmospheric chemistry and physics that carbon dioxide and water vapor trap solar heat. As sunlight falls on the earth's surface, it is re-emitted as infra-red light (the heat part of the spectrum), which is trapped by these gases.

b. It is now known scientifically as to what the Global Warming Potential (GWP - extent to which a gas traps solar heat) of these different gases are. Carbon dioxide has a lower GWP than methane gas, but as much more is emitted, it makes a much larger contribution to warming.

c. World signed its first Global Warming Treaty in 1992 at the Earth Summit in Rio de Janeiro, Brazil – , the treaty was called the UN Framework Convention on Climate Change (UNFCC)

d. Although this stated principles, there was no action demanded

e. The Kyoto Protocol (extension of treaty) was signed in 1997 and became effective in 2005 – it was an action plan with binding targets for some nations and non-binding targets for other nations

f. The Kyoto protocol commitment period began in 2008 and ended in 2012. The Doha Amendment (2012) to that protocol would have extended commitments but has not been ratified or signed by enough nations.

g. Few nations have achieved the targets they committed to.

h. December 2015: COP21 – or the twenty-first meeting of the Conference of Parties (that are signatories of the global warming treaty) that occurred in Paris. Descriptions elsewhere.

i. A big challenge lies ahead as firstly, how does one monitor each nation as to the commitments they made, and secondly, what will people with power in each nation, or what will their respective legislatures and executives do ?

j. One of the biggest battles brewing is the opposition by the most of the Republican Party to any movement or actions by US to contribute to a solution of the global warming problem.

k. To the credit of the executive branch of the US Government, as of December 2015, the US Environmental Protection Agency (USEPA) and the US President had done much by themselves, in spite of the opposition by Republican majorities in the Senate and the Congress.

l. They used the Supreme Court Ruling that Carbon Dioxide could be declared to be a pollutant whose emissions could be regulated. So the USEPA has drafted rules that would, say, limit carbon dioxide emissions from coal fired power plants (Clean Coal Initiative).

m. President Obama has come out with a Global Climate Change Initiative – this gives some hope, as the US is trying to do something, even though only at the executive level. This initiative invests in clean energy, promotes a global initiative to reduce deforestation and forest degradation globally ($ 1b investment), and helping low income countries to adapt to Climate Change.

4. <u>Major UN and Non-Governmental Actors & Movements</u>

In 1992, The United Nations (UN) played a key role in getting the nations of the world together at the Earth Summit, or the UN Conference on Environment & Development at Rio de Janeiro, Brazil. At that time I had organized an informal group in Chicago, called the Earth Summit Network, that attempted to apply pressure on the then Senior Bush US Administration to be more flexible at the Global Warming talks. Anyway, The US did sign the UN Framework Convention on Climate Change (UNFCC – or Global Warming treaty), the Biodiversity treaty, and Agenda 21 (or the global agenda for the 21st Century).
Some of the important actors in highlighting the problem of Global Warming have been as follows:

1. **<u>The UN based Intergovernmental Panel on Climate Change (IPCC</u>**), is a global organization that was set up by the World Meteorological Organization (WMO) and the UN Environment Programme (UNEP) in 1988 to provide governments with regular assessments of the scientific basis of climate change, its impacts, risks, and suggest strategies for mitigation (reducing emissions) and adaptation (adapting to current and future predicted changes). Hundreds of scientists from about 195 member countries participate in generating the assessments. IPCC has organized five major assessments on Climate Change since 1992, each assessment going further and further in confirming that human activity (or Anthropogenic emissions), have been significantly causing climate change. In addition to Al Gore (see below), the panel was awarded the Nobel Peace Prize as accepted by its then Chairman, Rajendra Pachauri. IPCC assessments provide extensive data and massive proof, and detailed assessments that firmly establish and describe the problem – for YOU THIS SHOULD PROVIDE CLEAR GUIDANCE NOT TO LISTEN TO THE DENIERS AND DOUBTERS, who dig up side studies and pseudo-scientific claims to throw doubts. For a description of IPCC assessments, visit the link below:

   https://www.ipcc.ch/report/ar5/

2. **<u>The Climate Reality Project – Al Gore</u>**
   Both as Vice-President, and later as private citizen, Al Gore highlighted the problem of Climate Change, and went around the world, providing information and promoting action. For his efforts, he received the Nobel Peace Prize is 2007, along with the IPCC. His most well-known 2006 book, "An Inconvenient Truth" is referenced below. Since then, he founded the Climate Reality Project, consisting of many motivated individuals, whose aim is to provide information and promote action on Climate Change.

   https://en.wikipedia.org/wiki/An_Inconvenient_Truth_(book)
   https://www.climaterealityproject.org/

3. **<u>350.Org – Bill McKibben</u>**
   350.org was formed by a number of university students in the US, along with the author Bill McKibben, who wrote a book on global warming. 350.org started organizing in 2008 to link

organizations globally, provide information, and to organize global events. The organization states that we need to reduce the concentration of Carbon Dioxide (CO_2) in the atmosphere from the current level of above 400 ppm (parts per million) to below 350 ppm, which many scientists say is needed to get escape the worst consequences of climate change – hence the name 350.org. See below for links.

Book – Bill McKibben, "Fight Global Warming Now," The Handbook for taking action in your community, 2007

http://350.org/

4. **People's Climate Action Movement - US**

   The Movement had organized a march on September 21, 2014, which demonstrated that there were many people that cared a lot about global warming, not just an environmental issue, but also as a movement for social and economic justice. The Movement has organized quite effectively, with the support of more than 245 groups globally, including groups such as the Sierra Club. On October 14, 2015, the Movement organized a nationwide call for action in the US, of which I participated in the march in Chicago – this was quite effective in mobilizing civil society in the US. On November 29, 2015, they organized a Global Climate March, the main one in Paris, had to be cancelled because of terror related security issues. The link is given below

http://peoplesclimate.org/

5. Solutions to Climate Change

It seems like the world appears to be aiming for limiting the average global surface temperature rise to no more than 2 Degrees Celsius (2 Deg. C – currently the temperature rise is about 0.6-0.7 deg. C). The 350.org organization would like the carbon dioxide concentration in atmosphere to be brought down to 350 ppm (part per million) from the current, which is over 400 ppm

The two degrees Celsius temperature rise limit can be achieved by the following:

   a. 60% - Energy Efficiency (Use of 60% less energy by)
      i. Our Cities, Our transportation, our industry, our buildings, our homes – redesigning our cities !
   b. 20% - Renewable Energy – clean energy
      i. Solar, Wind, Hydro, Tidal, etc.
   c. 20% - Bio-fuels – produced on non-agricultural land
      i. Of every kind – that keep recycling the Carbon

This overall strategy, if implemented immediately, will stabilize the CO_2 in atmosphere, and then reduce it to a level that will reduce the worst consequences of Climate Change, and allow Global Civilization to survive. It will give it the "breathing space" so that the human species can survive.

Also, fossil fuels are the biggest contributor to Climate Change. Coal is the biggest contributor, petroleum of oil is next, and natural gas, the least. One big part of the solution is that the use of fossil fuels should be reduced – coal first, petroleum or oil next, and natural gas last. It is estimated that 80% of the reserves of fossil fuels need to stay in the ground, in order to solve the problem.

HOW WE CAN ACHIEVE THIS

- **ENERGY EFFICIENCY** – This should be mandated and empowered
  - Use Fossil Fuels and their electricity more efficiently
  - Buildings designed with higher efficiency (Commercial and industrial) – LEED ratings, etc.
  - LEED – Leadership in Environmental and Energy- Efficient Design
    - These can be in silver, gold and platinum ratings
  - Homes – higher efficiency designs - save as well as produce energy
  - Transportation (Cars, Trucks and mix) & Air Transportation – Jet fuels
    - Improved fuel efficiency standards have been good, and saved, fuel, costs, been good for local environment, and for global warming
  - Industry – All mining, manufacturing and related activities can be converted to save energy and become low carbon
- **RENEWABLE ENERGY** – This should be encouraged
  - Solar PV – Electric – large scale electricity production by solar panels
  - Solar Thermal (including CSP) – heat and/or electricity
    - CSP is concentrated solar power, where mirrors that move with the sun concentrate the sunlight to a tower, the heat of which generates electricity
  - Wind Energy – Horizontal axis and Vertical axis turbines
    - Need extension of PTC – Production Tax Credit in US
  - Geothermal – Both for homes/buildings and hot geo-thermal for generating electricity from the equivalent of hot springs
  - Hydro-electric power – wherever water can be stored
    - This must be environmentally suitable and not in earthquake prone zones
  - Both rebates and tax credits should be renewed and extended
  - Most nations should implement incentives to encourage renewables
- **BIO-FUELS** – These should be encouraged
  - Crops on non-agricultural land
    - Crops on agricultural land should be discouraged
  - Algae and other similar technologies
  - Biomass Conversion – e.g. use of agricultural waste, etc.
- **OTHER – These should be encouraged**
  - Note: Not everyone agrees that nuclear energy is good, mainly because of its safety and long term toxicity/radioactivity concerns. However, it is include here as it does offer short term reductions in carbon
  - Nuclear – only if safety concerns are met
    - Otherwise, nuclear should be discouraged
  - CO_2 from exhaust stacks to Ethanol & Methanol (recycling carbon)

- This is a better way of capturing carbon before its release
- Waste and Wood to electricity (plantations based on sustainable forestry)
- Hydrogen as a storage medium – use it to store excess solar and wind energy, and then use in H2 generators or fuel cells to make electricity, to provide power or in transportation
- Energy Storage (Batteries) as a storage medium
  - These can store surplus energy, or store energy from solar and wind power, when it is not needed, for use later.

6. THE ROLE OF POLITICAL PRESSURE, MEDIA ACTIONS & ACTIVISM

The Paris Agreement has been negotiated – now it is time for you to tell your leaders wherever you live that they need to act, implement, facilitate, and fund. They need to start taking the actions that will help the transition to occur to a low carbon mode. It is important that YOU get activated and begin to help, work with or organize to apply political pressure in the nation in which you live. In the United States, because of the opposition that is coming mainly from members of the Republican Party, action on Climate Change has been strapped and the two legislatures, the Congress and the Senate have continued to place roadblocks in the path of progress towards solutions and actions to climate change. Legislators, national and state, and candidates for office, continue to deny the problem of climate change, and continue to argue that any efforts would discourage economic growth. Hence, it is important that citizens become activated, both to encourage those currently in power to take actions, pass legislations, and provide funding for solutions to climate change, including having their nation sign the Paris Agreement, and any similar agreements that may follow. Media actions have become extremely important in multiple ways to publicize events, or apply pressure. The two main approaches are:

1. **The Traditional Media Methods**: This includes the issuing of press releases to state positions, or publicize events, the sending of letters to the editor, and contacting radio and TV reporters and journalists, either to attend events, or to take personal interviews that are later broadcast. Sending regular letters in the mail, and making phone calls to the relevant people are also among traditional methods – this can be in terms of mass mailing campaigns or getting a large number of people to call.

2. **The Social Media Methods**: Because of the explosion of social media, like Facebook, Twitter and others, the use of social media has become very important and effective. The use of hashtags like #actonclimate that accompany any items or photos posted on social media are important. Short tweets with hashtags attached on Twitter to important public officials are one method. Similarly, one can send longer messages on Facebook with hashtags accompanying. This can be followed up by phone calls to important people, either the Governor of the state, or the state or national legislator - member of congress or senator, stating what you want them to do.

The Toolkit on the People's Climate Movement website provides very good and effective methods and resources for organizing for the above media actions:
http://peoplesclimate.org/toolkit/

Other forms of activism are to participate in rallies, and to use the radio and TV media by trying to get the message across, so that the programs of their radio and TV stations would provide coverage to you actions – sometimes with local, state, national or global impact.

Terminology

Climate Change; The change of the Earth's Climate by the warming of the atmosphere.

Global Warming: Another name for Climate Change, by which it directly refers to the heating of the atmosphere.

Greenhouse Gas: When sunlight falls to the Earth's surface, it is emitted back outwards mainly as infra-red light, or the heat part of the light spectrum. Greenhouse Gases in the atmosphere are those gases that trap some of this heat. The higher the amount of the greenhouse gas in the atmosphere, the more heat it traps. Examples are carbon dioxide, methane, ozone, water vapor, Chloro-fluoro-carbons (CFCs that damage the ozone layer, that protects us from ultra-violet light), etc.

Global Warming Potential (GWP): this is the potential or capability of a gas to trap heat. For example carbon dioxide, that is generated by the burning of fossil fuels, has a much lower GWP than methane (that is emitted by many sources – including biodegradation of organic matter, and when extracting natural gas)

Fossil Fuel Comparisons: The burning of coal emits the largest amount of carbon dioxide per unit of heat (BTU – British Thermal Unit) generated. The next is line is petroleum based products (gasoline, diesel, etc). The fuel that emits the least carbon dioxide when you burn it is Natural Gas.

7. Action Guides

A. What Can I Do in my Personal and Family Life ?

- **Heat & Cool your home efficiently**
  - Furnace & Air Conditioner Efficiency – costs only $1,000-2,000 more for the average home
  - When you need to, get the highest efficiency furnace (96-98%)
  - Get an air conditioner that is at least 16 SEER rating or higher (SEER – Seasonal Energy Efficiency Ratio)
- **Install Energy Efficient Lighting – CFLs and LEDs**
  - Use CFL bulbs to begin with 23W is equivalent of 100W incandescent
  - Use LED light bulbs – these are even more efficient
  - LED bulbs last ten times longer than the original incandescent bulbs on the average – so total cost including electricity is much less.
- **Buy only Energy Efficient Appliances**
  - Do not buy anything that is not Energy Star Rated
  - Demand to know the energy consumption guide and compare to other competitive appliances – buy the most energy efficient appliance that you can afford.
- **Engage in Energy Production at Home or Business?**
  - Solar PV (Photo-Voltaic - Electricity), Solar Thermal (Heat) and Geothermal (Saving) ? These can save you big on your utility costs – get a contractor to do a site survey and give you a quote.
  - Consider adding Solar PV panels on your roof or on a pole in the backyard. Solar panel costs have come down from $4-5/watt to about $1-2/watt in 2015 (system costs from about $ 9/watt to about $ 5/watt today)
  - Consider Solar thermal panels that do hot water heating – these cost less than Solar PV panels and the money is earned back sooner.
- If you are affluent enough to build your own house, then make it a **zero energy or positive energy home**, that is built energy efficiently, uses daylighting principles and uses a combination of Solar PV, Solar thermal, and geothermal (heat pump, with pipes buried in the ground)
- **Air Travel – See what you can do to cut down on Flying miles ?**
- **Driving** – When you can, buy and begin to drive a high mpg or Hybrid Car ?
  - Next time you buy a car insist on high mileage, consider buying a hybrid or an electric car
- **Food** – Cut down on the amount of beef, pork and other animal products, as much as you can. Eat Organic and, if you are not already, consider becoming a vegetarian. The animal products diet does much, directly and indirectly, to contribute to carbon emissions (cutting down of forests, animal ranches, large amounts of land and agricultural products used as animal feed, etc.)
- **Recycling & Composting** – Recycle everything that you can – participate in recycling from your homes, businesses and communities – encourage and apply pressure for all levels of government

to recycle and facilitate recycling programs. Compost as much of your kitchen waste as you can, and use or give as fertilizer, and participate in programs if yard wastes are picked up and sent for landfill composting?

- **Have you run the <u>Carbon Footprint Calculator</u> to see what YOUR contribution to Global warming is ?**

  CALCULATE YOUR CARBON FOOTPRINT !
- **Many available – Run one by Nature Conservancy**
- **http://www.nature.org/greenliving/carboncalculator/index.htm**
  - Calculates one's total Green House Gas Emissions
  - Lamba Family (2 people) = 36 tons of CO_2 equivalent/yr.
  - US Average (2 people) = 53 tons of CO_2 equivalent/yr.
  - World Average (2 people) = 11 tons of CO_2 equivalent/yr.
  - <u>World Average Needs to be = 5 tons of CO_2 equivalent/yr.</u> to meet the limit of no more than 2 degrees Celsius temperature rise
  - <u>See what you can do to bring down your carbon footprint</u>

Actions You can Take Out There !
Community, State, National & International

Many cities, counties, districts, states and nations have already begun to plan and implement energy efficiency actions, or reduce their carbon footprint. If yours has not, then begin to apply pressure that they do so (the word "encourage" has been used below). If funding is a problem, then try and find a way so that international or national mechanisms can help your local governments. In many cases, local and national level organizations may already be active in many of these activities, so the best strategy may be to support and participate in their activities. In some cases, it may be suitable to submit petitions, and demand that currently available funds be used for solar and (vertical axis) wind generators be installed on all public buildings.

B. In our Cities, Counties, Districts and States

a. Encourage Carbon efficient operations – buildings and activities – energy efficiency

b. Encourage green transportation, hybrid buses, natural gas buses, electric light rail, etc.

    i. Use as often as you can

c. Encourage local bicycle and pedestrian transportation – bikeways and pedestrian ways or sidewalks should be encouraged – use as often as you can

d. Show up at weekly city hall meetings and environmental commission meetings, or legislative meetings, whatever is available locally

e. Encourage renewable energy and energy efficient lighting – like solar/wind powered street lights

f. Encourage the installation of solar and wind energy (here the vertical axis wind turbines may be most suitable for urban areas) in all existing public buildings

C. In our States or Provinces – Additional Actions

Since many states have legislatures, elected governments and elected leaders, then there can be added actions that you can encourage. **To provide an example, in the state of Illinois in the US,** legislators have introduced the "Clean Jobs Bill" in the Illinois state's house and senate legislatures. This Bill if passed, would build a clean energy generating system. It would: (1) Increase Energy Efficiency so as to reduce energy demand by 20% by 2025, by home and building retrofits, access to energy efficient appliances, and allow non-utility energy efficiency providers to deliver energy efficiency services, (2) Increase us of Renewable Energy – raise the current Renewable Portfolio Standard (RPS) to 25% by 2025, and 35% by 2030 – RPS requires all utilities to produce that percentage of their energy supplied through renewable energy, and (3) Pursuing Market based strategies to reduce carbon pollution and create jobs – implement a market mechanism to limit carbon pollution.

The other initiative that is being pushed in Illinois, is for the state to implement the **Clean Power Plan developed by the US President and the USEPA (US Environmental Protection Agency) in June 2014**. This plan proposed new carbon pollution standards for power plants – this provides a strong incentive for utilities to move toward renewable energy and energy conservation. For Illinois, this means improving power plants' operational efficiency, encouraging low cow carbon energy producers like solar and wind, improving energy efficiency of homes and buildings, and use of nuclear and natural gas plants to reduce the scope for high carbon emitting coal plants. For Illinois, this would mean reducing the carbon emission rate for power plants from 1,895 lbs. per mega watt-hour (lb./MWH) in 2012, to 1,271 lb./MWH by 2030. If implemented in Illinois, this plan would mean big increases in energy efficiency, general pollution and carbon pollution, while creating an estimated additional 32,000 jobs on top of the 100,000 jobs already engaging those employed in renewables. See link below

http://www3.epa.gov/airquality/cpptoolbox/illinois.pdf

Wherever you live in the world, encourage your local state governments to take up and implement similar actions – not just in words, but in actions – <u>demand proof</u> that they are doing it. not just say that they will do it.

D. National Level Actions

The most important message that you need to get to your national leaders is to make sure they sign the Paris Agreement, and any following agreements. Next, they need to make sure that they implement what they promised to do as a part of their NDCs (Nationally Determined Contributions). The US president and the executive branch of Government has been doing the most it can under the circumstances:

1. Clean Power Plan: In August 2015, the US Government announced the Clean Power Plan, that would reduce the carbon pollution from power plants 32% by the year 2030, and increase renewable energy (mainly solar and wind) production by 30% by the year 2030. This main y effects Coal fired Power Plants, which will have to reduce their pollution, and at the same time encourage renewable energy. This should have significant health benefits, and while it may reduce jobs in existing power plants, will increase jobs in renewable energy production.

2. Clean Energy Federal Activities: The US Government has done much in terms of solar and wind energy production on lands under its control, and encouraged and conducted training of veterans and others in solar energy, and funded clean energy projects. Investments in clean energy technology range from bio-fuels, and nuclear energy to clean coal. Its plans include a doubling of wind and solar energy production nationwide, and reaching 100MW of renewable energy production on federally subsidized housing by 2020. The Department of Defense plans to have 3 Giga-watts of renewable energy on its sites by 2025.

3. Energy Efficiency: In 2011 the government announced the fuel economy standards for model year 2014-2018 heavy duty trucks, buses and vans, and passenger car fuel economy standard has been set at 54.5 miles per gallon by 2025. Much has been done through the Better Building Challenge to increase the efficiency of buildings.

4. Adaptation: The government has assessed the impacts of climate change, rebuilding and learning from superstorm Sandy, helping farmers to maintain agricultural productivity and reducing the risks of droughts and wild fires

5. Internationally: The US is working with other countries in Climate Change. Other nations such as UK, Nordic countries and Netherlands joined the US in an initiative to end public financing of coal fired power plants overseas. The US Department of Energy has initiated a Clean Energy Ministerial, so that at a high level there can be discussions on how to scale up clean energy and energy efficiency. The US is leading a Clean Air Coalition with about 100 partners including 46 nations aiming at reducing emissions of methane gas, HFCs (Hydro-Fluoro-Carbons – that destroy the Ozone layer), and black carbon. In 2014, the US Federal Government contributed $ 3 billion to a Green Climate Fund aimed at helping developing nations – this encouraged others so that the fund now has $ 10 billion in it.

https://www.whitehouse.gov/climate-change

The need for Political Activism Within Your Nation

The biggest challenge facing the USA is how to get the legislative sector of government to go from being against actions for climate change, to that of being a solid supporter of actions to solve the climate change problem. This will require a lot of activism at all levels to make this happen. At each location, wherever people live, citizens should demand responsiveness on this issue, discourage those candidates for office who are clearly opposed to action and support those that are clearly for climate change solutions and actions.

E. Global Actions

While the main focus of climate change may need to be on those nations that are making the biggest contributions to carbon emissions, it is important to realize that all nations and all the people of the world live and breathe the same atmosphere. Carbon emissions in one nation spread out and occupy the whole atmosphere. So, one nation, or a small of group of nations, that continue to increase their carbon emissions can wipe out the benefits of the emissions reductions by all the other nations. Hence, an effective global agreement is very important. The Paris Agreement is a good start ! Now the challenge is that of monitoring each nation and making sure that they implement the actions they committed to as part of their NDCs (Nationally Determined Commitments).

The following is a list of countries with their annual Carbon Dioxide gas emissions in 2013, as obtained from Wikipedia in January, 2015.

Nation or Category	CO2 Emissions (MT)*	Emissions per Capita (T) **
World	35,669	5
China	10,540	7.6
United States	5,334	16.5
European Union	3,415	6.7
India	2,341	1.8
Russia	1,766	12.4
Japan	1,278	10.1
Germany	767	9.3
Global Shipping	624	-
Iran	618	7.9
South Korea	610	12.3
Canada	565	15.9
Brazil	501	2.5
Saudi Arabia	494	16.8
Global Aviation	492	-
Mexico	456	3.7
Indonesia	452	1.8
United Kingdom	415	6.5
Australia	409	17.3
South Africa		7.4

	392	
Turkey	353	4.7
Italy	337	5.5
France	323	5
Poland	298	7.8
* MT - Millions of Metric Tons of CO2		
** T - Metric Tons, or Tonnes		
Ref.: Wikipedia - Carbon Emissions by Country		

https://en.wikipedia.org/wiki/List_of_countries_by_carbon_dioxide_emissions

The top 10 emitter nations, emit about 68.2% of the total. This list does not include other greenhouse gases, such as methane (this emitted by landfills, and cattle). Also, this lists only direct emissions from the burning of fossil fuels and by activities such as cement manufacture, but do not include changes in land use, land use change and forestry (which can affect the absorption of carbon dioxide).

The Need for Global Activism

The first part of Global Activism is for YOU to be applying pressure on the major emitter nations of the world, and your own nation to sign the Paris Agreement. Next, although each nation will submit information the performance of each nation, and its performance will be recorded, monitored and reported by the Climate Change Secretariat at Geneva, Switzerland, it is important that you and every global citizen to pay attention to this and put pressure on their respective nations, and on the large emitter nations to demonstrate that they are meeting or exceeding their commitments. Participate in the organizations in your own country, or that of organizations globally that you have access to so as to make this happen. The Climate Reality Project and 350.org are two such organizations. Greenpeace is another global organization that is active, and has had a proposed plan for solving to climate change problem. At this point is important that YOU DEMAND action by the leaders of your and every major emitter nation, and hold them ACCOUNTABLE!

8. Implementations of Global Warming Solutions – The Principles

It will take every trick in the trade for humans to solve the problem of climate change. Now, when we install infrastructure or buildings or homes or factories or transportation pathways, the longer term the nature of the project, the more energy efficient and low carbon it needs to be. Why ? Because it is going to be consuming energy and emitting carbon for a long time. Then, when we install a new plant or method of energy production, it is important that after it is installed, it should be a zero carbon or a low carbon production mode. Why? Because it is going to be producing energy and carbon for a long time – many decades at least. It should be excusable to use fossil fuels in its production and installation, if it is a onetime contribution to carbon emissions, because the long term benefits over decades will outweigh the carbon contribution – especially if it is going to produce or consume energy forever. Still, every effort and technique should be used to minimize the use of materials and energy in producing and installing what we do. You can find a more detailed description of these alternatives in the book by the author titled, "Rethinking Progress – Towards a Creative Transformation of Global Society".

Several nations, including the US have made fuel efficiency standards for cars mandatory. This has not only saved drivers a lot of money, but it has resulted in less local pollution, and less carbon emissions. In the US, it appears to have been overwhelmed by the increasing number of vehicles and miles driven.

A. Energy Efficient & Net Energy Producing Homes & Buildings – Make them Mandatory

Now, we need to demand that our nations make mandatory the following: (1) Builders and others should only be able to build homes if they are the most energy efficient and produce as much or more energy by clean energy methods (wind or solar), than they consume – on a net basis. The homes can still be tied to the grid, and draw or feedback energy to the grid, and hence have a reliable set-up for energy production, supply and use, and (2) Builders, architects and construction companies, should only be able to build the highest energy efficiency buildings. Some sections of the building industry in the US use the LEED rating standards (LEED stands for Leadership in Energy & Environmental Design), established by the US Green Building Council. However, this is not good enough. Building should be required by design to use less energy and whatever energy they do use, again as for homes, they should be required to produce as much or more energy by renewable energy methods than they consume. Big support and incentives should be given to given to energy efficient retrofits – not just energy efficiency measures such as insulation and windows, but actual partial and wholescale reconstruction to save energy.

All homes should be required to and helped to become net producers of energy. This can be done in many places by the use of solar PV and wind energy for generating electricity, solar thermal for hot water and space heating, and geothermal (or heat pumps) that rely on the constant temperature in the ground and system of pipes buried underground to extract or dump heat into the ground.

B. <u>Our Cities Should be Energy Efficient & Low Carbon</u>

Our cities need to be transformed into low carbon cities, where energy production, energy use and transportation are all low carbon. As in Section A above, all homes and buildings in the cities need to be retrofitted, so that they not only produce energy (solar or wind), but also are retrofitted to reduce energy use while enhancing comfort. The transportation methods and infrastructure need to be totally transformed so as to be clean and low carbon. All existing modes such as cars, taxis, motorcycles and buses need to be required to be the most fuel efficient – fuel efficiency standards should be raised and continue to be raised, has been done in the US for a few decades now.

All new cities need to totally designed and built as eco-cities, that are built like eco-systems in that they recycle all their water, treat and reuse all solid waste as fertilizer, have water and forest ecosystems comingling with the city, and transportation is such that residents have many transportation choices – with the infrastructure such that people can walk, bike, take mass transit, use electric bikes and electric cars, and use cars only when needed – but that too, so that many areas of the city can do without cars, and do not have the noise, pollution or carbon intensiveness of fossil fuel using cars. Combining architecture and ecology, or arcology* is a new science and technology where 3D structures can enable relatively large numbers of people to have easy access to living, working, educational, health facilities, creative and recreational areas. Also, roads would not be the unsafe barriers they are today, artificially dividing up the cities into smaller isolated segments that can only be accessed by cars.

C. <u>Clean, Renewable and Alternative Energy Production</u>

Much progress has occurred in such production. However, now every effort should be made to engage in large scale and small scale renewable energy production, such as Solar, Wind, Geothermal (use of hot temperatures in the earth), hydro (done ecologically), Bio-fuels (grown on non-agricultural land), and energy production from natural wastes (wood chips, agricultural waste, etc.) in low smoke and low pollution mode. The areas of the world that are deficit in energy production are also areas that receive much larger amount of solar energy each day, and through the year. Use of higher technology like solar tracking (making sure that the panel is directly facing the sun at all times during the day), higher efficiency panels, and storage of energy when it is being produced but not immediately needed. Energy can be stored on large battery systems that get charged when the energy is being produced, and then discharged to provide energy when clouds stop sunlight, or during the night when the sun is not shining.

One of the problems that occurs is that solar or wind energy is often best produced far from where electric transmission lines are located, or far from cities where most of the consumption occurs, or at a time when it is not needed. One energy storage means that needs to be considered, because it will provide much greater flexibility, is the conversion of surplus energy into Hydrogen and Oxygen by splitting water by electrolysis, or by any advanced technology method that enables hydrogen to be generated. The hydrogen thus produced can be transported by truck, pipeline or rail to locations where it can be stored, and then used to produce electricity, either by combustion or through the use of large fuel cells. It is this, more than anything else that will lead to a hydrogen based economy – use hydrogen as a storage medium.

D. Industry that Recycles its Carbon

Carbon sequestration had received a great deal of attention many years back. This required actually burying carbon dioxide under pressure in geological formations. This has proven to be very difficult and expensive, with the dangers of earthquakes and no proof that this would work. Another technique that is gaining promise, which all industries which are emitting carbon dioxide from their stacks, should use, is that of converting the carbon dioxide into ethanol or other petroleum type products. This process requires microbes that have an affinity for "eating" carbon dioxide and converting it into ethanol and other chemicals through the process of fermentation. This process has actually taken off and is being implemented on an industrial scale. What this would do is essentially recycle the carbon, so that the carbon dioxide would not end up in the atmosphere, and at the same time would provide additional energy as ethanol. For example, a company called LanzaTech, located in Skokie, Illinois, uses this to capture carbon and reuse it, by producing ethanol from it.

E. Repairing and Restoring Carbon Sinks – Our Global Eco-systems

The global ecosystems were undergoing some destruction as the we humans expanded all over our Earth. Civilization after civilization collapsed when they exceeded the capacity of their immediately available environment, and their natural resources degraded through overuse. The colonizing of the rest of the world by mostly European nations, led to large scale deforestation, as the wood and timber resources. The Americas, North and South, were largely afforested before colonization – and became rapidly deforested in a few centuries, as forest were cut down for fuel and agriculture.

The global ecosystems have been in the process of rapidly increasing destruction since the start of the Industrial Revolution a couple of centuries ago. Our beautiful planet Earth is being rapidly converted into an ugly planet. Its forests are rapidly being destroyed, arid lands are being turned into desert, deserts are expanding, coral reefs are being bleached and are dying due to hotter temperatures and pollution, coastal ecosystems (like mangrove swamps) are being destroyed, Mountains and hills are being denuded and ruined by mudslides, our Earth is being rapidly poisoned by radioactive, toxic and chemical waste, our fisheries are being over fished, our soils are losing fertility and depth, wildfires followed by landslides are destroying many areas, and hurricanes, cyclones, tornadoes and coastal storms are damaging many developed areas.

Most of these global ecosystems, including our oceans, are Carbon sinks – that is, they absorb carbon dioxide. However, the destruction of ecosystems, and increasing carbon dioxide and temperatures of our oceans, are decreasing the ability of these global ecosystems. The biggest task ultimately is to lower the concentration of carbon dioxide in the atmosphere.

We have to begin the process of not only repairing but totally rejuvenating all of our ecosystems as follows:

1. Forests & land-based Ecosystems: Besides proceeding to protect all rainforests, <u>we need to plan for a total reforestation of the Earth</u> – ALL nations, including the developed ones. This plan must be tied to the needs of local populations for extractive strategies from standing forests – i.e. people living in or near the forests can take materials, food, fruit, etc. but mostly leave tress intact – or keep planting if they cut down. We need to use the principles of sustainable forestry or landscape restoration – for the latter see efforts of the Global Partnership for Landscape Restoration. A similar effort needs to be mounted to restore the other land areas of the Earth, especially the deserts and arid areas, so they can continue to support life and the local human populations.

2. We need to move rapidly to protect the remaining Coral Reefs of the world. For this major programs are needed that would minimize the bleaching of coral reefs due to climate change, help protect them from land and sea based pollution, damage by shipping and mining activities, and provide nurseries that help preserve endangered coral, plant and animal species, for reef restoration. For examples of this, refer to the work of the Coral Restoration Foundation and the NOAA (The US National Oceanic and Atmospheric Administration) Coral Reef Restoration Program, and the Damage Assessment, Remediation and Restoration Program.

3. At the same time, similar activities are needed to restore, coastal, mountain and hill ecosystems, the river watersheds, and the polar ecosystems (Arctic and Antarctic).

F. <u>Reforming & Restoring Agriculture, Horticulture, and other "Cultures"</u>

One of the ways to improve the productive capacity and the carbon absorption capacity of land masses, is to restore the productive capacity and fertility of land masses that are used to grow food, fuel and medicine. We need to move away from heavily fuel, fertilizer, pesticide, herbicide and water intensive forms of agriculture that are degrading the fertility and quality of the soils, while producing environmental damage, and a poisoning of water masses. We need to move to methods of agriculture that are more organic, use less of these materials, use less water, and use more of the traditional varieties of seeds, or at least a greater variety of crop types, as compared with the mono-culture crops that can be more prone to large scale failures due to disease or insects. The processes of natural or organic farming will also restore the fertility of soils, which are being depleted by "green revolution" agriculture.

G. Producing a Healthy, Happy, Sustainable & Productive Life for ALL

Currently, major sections of the world are either left out of the global production and consumption processes or work very hard and earn very little, with most of the benefits being appropriated by 1% of society. The amounts that are invested, if large, employ very few people and often do not go to meet the basic needs of people, but are there to meet the high consumption wants of the top earning part of society.

The kinds of progress that are being followed are leading to increasing degradation in the livelihoods, basic needs fulfilment and basic health and well-being of major sections of the world's population. Rather than progress that just leads to increasing wealth for the few, climate change and the destruction of global ecosystems, alternative methods and types of productive activity are needed, that directly lead to a healthy, happy, sustainable and productive life style for all of the world's population.

Ways need to be found to do all of the tasks described above – renewable energy production, energy efficiency, agriculture, etc., in such a way that it involves much larger numbers of people – so that there is greater ownership, employment, income and basic needs consumption by much larger numbers of people. This will strengthen the demand side of nations, so that there will be larger numbers of people that have a higher purchasing power – so this might actually benefit some current businesses, except for those involved in fossil fuel based industries.

Large corporations produce their products in ways that require less and less labor, and yet sell these all of the people. One innovation would be that there be a direct link between earning employment and consumption for that economic activity. That will ensure that the producers are also consumers of the products of others close by and that they are involved in economic activity, where they earn locally and consume locally – or at least the produce others, who operate similarly. One of the main ways this can happen, is for local productivity based on access to local raw materials, is directly tied to local consumption. Many nations, including now the US, are requiring local content – i.e. a major part of the imported product needs to be made within the country. In the same way, a localized region can require that this be the case,

Currently, the large food corporations use large mono-cultural crops to produce processed food products in automated factories that employ few people. A major opportunity is for the development of agricultural products based industries that enable people at decentralized locations to process more of their produce and sell the processed food and other products to all markets – this should generate skill development, employment, finances and ownership. These alternative production technologies are available – what one needs are larger corporations that produce the capital machinery for these smaller scale localized production.

There also needs to be a transition strategy for businesses and people currently involved in the fossil fuel industry. There needs to be incentives and assistance provided so that the businesses transition to more planetary friendly activities and the people employed in them are trained and relocated to the low carbon and zero carbon activities of the future.

9. Imagining a Post Global Warming World

So let us imagine what our planet Earth will look like after we have successfully solved the problem of Climate Change and avoided its worst consequences. First, for sure, we will still have a planet ravaged by Climate Change, where everyone has adapted to it. However, the planet will begin to look a lot more like it can better support life.

1. The Earth will look much greener as all land and sea based ecosystems will have been not only restored but also rejuvenated (better that before).
2. The cities would have been transformed into beautiful green areas – healthy, productive and joyful.
3. Our agricultural areas, rather than filled with large areas of mono-cultural crops (like a carpet of only one color), will look like a beautiful mosaic, where many different crops and crop varieties are grown. The land looks much greener and more interesting and varied, and supports a different agricultural economy, that is more ecological, requires less inputs and resources, keeps improving the fertility of the soil, and supports the food and livelihood needs of all of the population.
4. Not much land will have been lost to sea level rise, as the worst would have been averted.
5. Global Society will have learned to produce all of their energy from zero carbon activity (solar, wind, geothermal, etc.) or that where carbon is recycled.
6. We will have learned to meet our many needs (buildings, homes, transportation, appliances, etc.) by very energy efficient means – using much less energy to do what we had done before.
7. Rather than produce things at one location and transport them all over the world, which was wasteful from an energy standpoint, we will have everyone engaged in a productive and creative activity, with productive activities all over.

8. All of the ecosystems of our Earth (that provide its life support systems), the forests, the coral reefs, the coastal, mountainous and watershed ecosystems, will all have been, not only restored but also rejuvenated (healthier than before), enabling the human species and all of the rest of living species to thrive for millions of years to come !

10. <u>Reading Resources for Climate Change</u>

1. Soleri, Paolo, "Arcology: The City in the Image of Man," Phoenix, Arizona, Bridgewood Press, 1999.
   Describes how cities can be transformed, or new cities can be designed that combine architecture, urban design and ecology to transition to cities that are green, beautiful, clean, with low levels of pollution and noise.

2. Lamba, Harinder S., "Rethinking Progress – Towards a Creative Transformation of Global Society", Daanish Books, Delhi and Patna, 2005.
   The first half of the book describes the major environment, development, financial, and progress issues faced by global society. The second half of the book describes how we can transform to the post Global Warming world, not only environmentally and developmentally, bit also financially, with a changed more beneficial economic emphasis, and the nature of democratic institutions from local to global that help transition to the new way of doing things, and strengthen the processes that lead to both environmental rejuvenation and a healthier, productive, and happier life for all.

3. Laurie David, "Stop Global Warming," Fulcrum Publishing, 2006 and 2008.
   Laurie gives some description of the science and how he got involved. He then advances the case that global warming is the defining global civil rights issue of our time, and what we can do about it. He urges recycling or the avoidance in the use of many things. Some startling statistics – Americans throw away 100 billion plastic bags every year (14 plastic bags = driving average car one mile)! Paper bags use 4 times more energy, but only 20% recycled. Americans buy 25 billion single serve plastic bottles every year, and throw 2.5 million every hour!
   www.stopglobalwarming.org

4. Tim Flannery, "Now or Never", Atlantic Monthly Press, 2009
   While focusing on global warming, he points to the problem of coal. One issue he highlights is the solutions that can be achieved by better managing livestock farming. He advocates the case for reducing the numbers of sheep and cattle. Although methane gas is emitted by animals in smaller quantities (than carbon dioxide), it has 25 times more global warming potential – but also that methane breaks down and 2/3rds is gone in 10 years. Better rangeland management could pull out one gigatonne of carbon from atmosphere per year. Brief write-ups by Peter Singer and Bill McKibben 350.org.

5. Roger Pielke, Jr., "The Climate Fix," Basic Books, 2010
   Roger indicates that data on losses incurred from natural disasters and their incidence – trends appear to be exponential upwards. He points to the tendency of vested interests to talk about, "What we know for sure, but it ain't so!" This refers to the denial of something even when all the evidence stares you in the face. He describes decarbonization of the global economy and decarbonization policies around the world. He points out that climate policy went off course due to politicization, and the first steps to be taken back in the right direction.

6. Al Gore, "An Inconvenient Truth," Rodale Press, 2006.

    To Al Gore goes the credit of keeping Climate Change on the global agenda, both when he was a US Vice-President and thereafter. His book provides ample evidence and photos that document that in photos. His book points to not only the science of Climate Change but also highlights many of the solutions.

7. James Hansen, "Storms of My Grandchildren," 2009

    "The truth about the coming Climate Catastrophe and our last chance to save humanity"
    James' book highlights what happened in the US political arena in the 1990s, relating to Climate Change. His book points to the dangers of ignoring the problem. From 1981-2013 he headed the NASA Goddard Institute for Space Studies, New York City. He discusses the level of carbon dioxide to which the world should aim, so as to avoid the most serious consequences on Climate Change. He points out that the planet Venus is a similar size to planet Earth, but being closer to the sun, the water has boiled off, and the atmosphere has a very high concentration of carbon dioxide – leading to a runaway greenhouse effect – one that feeds on itself.

8. Gary Braasch, "How Global Warming is Changing the World," 2007

    With an afterword by Bill McKibben
    Gary points to the effect that climate change is having on the frozen parts of the planet. He emphasizes that climate change is not in the distant future, but that we are seeing it today. He argues for a safer, cleaner and cooler world than where we are headed.

BIO OF THE AUTHOR

Harinder (Hari) Lamba considers himself to be an engineer with a social and environmental conscience. He is an engineer by profession, working in the transportation industry, and has designed parts of railway locomotives and encouraged the process of innovation. He has a bachelor's degree in Aeronautical Engineering from India and Master's and Ph.D. degrees in Engineering Mechanics from the University of Illinois at Urbana- Champaign, USA.

 He has done volunteer work on environmental, development, high speed rail and social issues with non-governmental organizations and groups focusing on the US, South Asia, India and the World. His interests include developing new products, renewable energy to solve the world's energy problems, music, poetry, and literature. He is the author of the book, "Rethinking Progress – Towards a Creative Transformation of Global Society", Daanish Books, New Delhi, India, 2005. Can order book through website www.renewtechs.com.

The first half of the book describes the terrible environmental mess that we are in, in terms of global warming, ozone layer depletion, ecosystem destruction, radioactive waste, toxic waste, air/water/soil pollution, municipal solid waste, and destruction of the fertility of our soils. It then goes on to describe the biography of our Planet Earth, which describes the incredible process by which our planet has not only evolved, but has also supported life. Fossil fuels that took hundreds of millions of years to remove carbon from the atmosphere are within a matter of a couple of hundred years being released fast and furiously into the atmosphere. For all of the miracles of technology, the world has not led to better life, and has actually worsened conditions for major sections of the world's population – what the author calls the failure of development. Both because of environment and development problems, it is important that we question the mode of our progress and chart a different course.

The second half of that book outlines such a different course - ideas for the sustainable transformation of global society: All human activities need to be transformed - our cities, transportation, industry, agriculture, economics, politics, local to global governance, and the repair and rejuvenation of global ecosystems, and the life support systems of the planet. All of our activities not only have to be converted into lower or low carbon activities, but many new activities have to either low carbon or zero carbon, so that we can solve the most desperate problem of Climate Change. Simultaneously, this has to be done in such a way that it shows and implements ways in which all of the human population is able to enjoy a full and sustainable life, healthy, adequate, and joyful!

He recently published a collection of about 28 poems about the enjoyment of nature and the beauty of our planet Earth. The poem book is titled, **"Our Only Home – Poems for our Planet Earth," 2014.**, and is available in Kindle format on Amazon. The poem book emphasizes that our Earth is **BEAUTIFUL** It also emphasizes that nowhere else in our Solar System are the conditions favorable for life, and that beyond our solar system the time to travel is many light years, which is not practical to reach and colonize. So, our dear planet Earth is our only home. Just like this book, much of my poetry in that Poem Book belongs to a recently developing tradition called, "Verse Journalism", that seeks to add a feeling of responsibility and purpose – something that is urgently needed if we are develop alternatives to our current ways of doing things – whether it is in energy, or habitats, or transportation, or agriculture, or industry, or – last but not least – saving our dying global ecosystems, and then rejuvenating them.

He is also in the process of publishing a book, "History of Our Earth & Our Role in its Future," a poem starting with the Big Bang to the present, and with beautiful watercolors recording the history of our beautiful Earth. This book describes in a fun and colorful way how Earth was born as a part of the solar system, as a molten ball, and the amazing journey over nearly 4.6 billion years to cool, develop the seas, evolve life, go from no oxygen to oxygen through photosynthesis, remove carbon from the atmosphere and store it in fossils and buried carboniferous forests. As the atmosphere cooled by reducing carbon, life as we know evolved as plants, trees, insects, and animals, and finally us – the human species. It is hoped that that poem book will not only be enjoyed by adults, but also be enjoyed and recited by school children – a fun way to look at a serious topic. This book should be available in print format or Create Space and in Kindle format on Amazon, after April of 2016.

Besides his commitment to finding solutions to global warming, he is committed to developing new products that will help the generation of renewable energy, and in helping bring about a transformation in all aspects of human activity so as to solve the problems of climate change, environmental rejuvenation, and helping all of the people of the world enjoy a wholesome, sustainable, productive and happy life. Look for more books, efforts and products from the author that make this happen.